This is a stringed instrument.

violin
/vieulin/

Parts of the instrument:

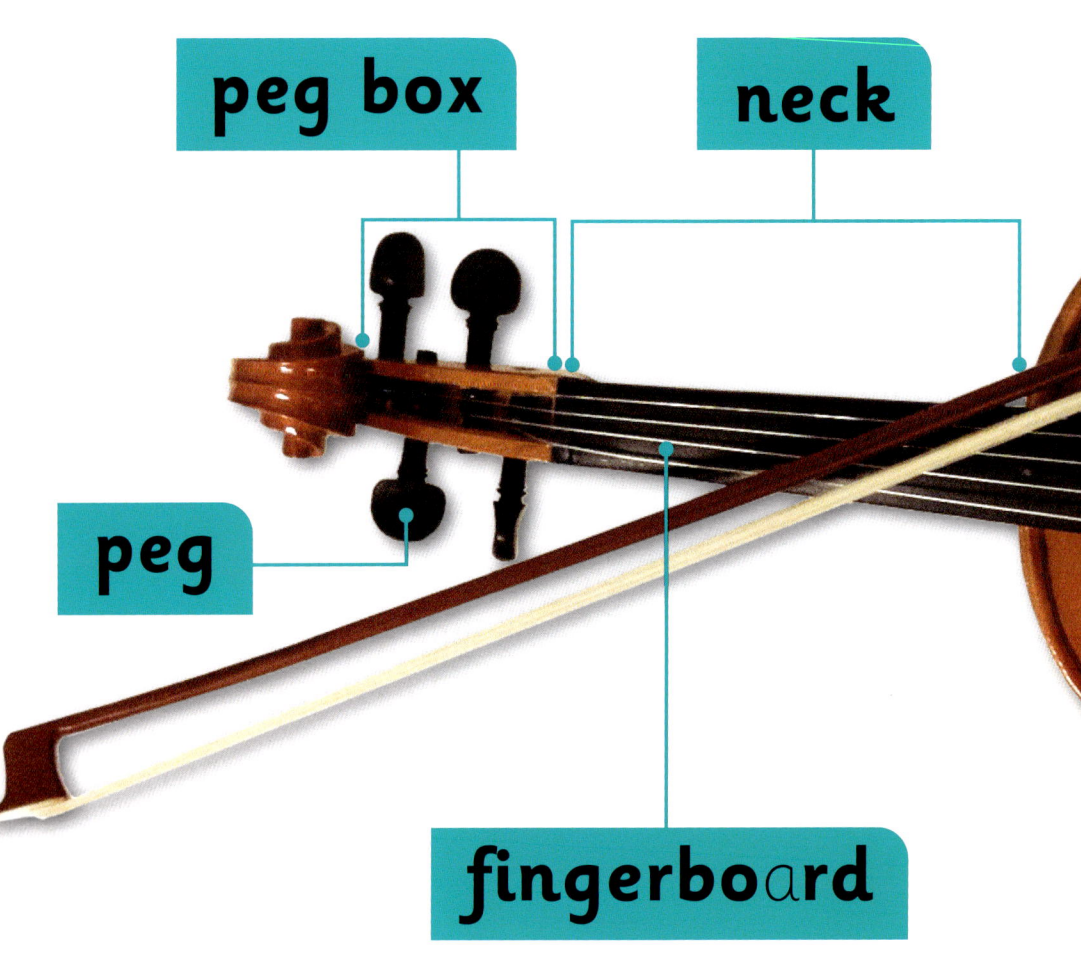

peg box

neck

peg

fingerboard

strings

chin rest

It is tucked under the chin.

Fingers press the strings onto the fingerboard.

the fingerboard

The strings are rubbed
to get the sound.

The strings can be plucked as well.

Stringed instruments can be electric, too.